Acknowledgements

My thanks go to my participants; without you this work would quite literally not exist. To my supervisor, Dr Lucy Pickering, for their encouragement, guidance, support and, most of all, understanding throughout this. Without them it wouldn't have happened!

Contents

ACADEMIA LUNARE

The Austerity Cure:
The Impact of Benefit Sanctions on Mental Health

Degree of Master of Research (MRes) Sociology & Research Methods, School of Social & Political Sciences, University of Glasgow.

Michelle K Jamieson

Academia Lunare
LUNA PRESS PUBLISHING

1. Abstract

Background: The impact of benefit sanctions on mental health and self-care has been little debated, yet there is clear evidence linking them to mental, physical, and social damage. Talking to people who have experienced this situation can provide useful information, including the factors that compound poor mental health, and subsequent self-care choices. This information may help others in the same position.

Design & Methods: This qualitative study aims to explore the experience of living in Glasgow with a complex mental health condition during a benefit sanction. Individuals (n=7) who had experienced this were interviewed about their experiences. The semi-structured interviews were audio recorded and then transcribed verbatim and analysed using interpretative phenomenological analysis, and framed by T.H. Marshall's Theory of Citizenship and Psychologists Against Austerity's framework.

Results & Conclusions: Three main themes emerged from the interviews: 1. Life Lived in Shades of Grey, 2. Good Citizen, Bad Citizen, and, 3. Helping Hands. Participants described a range of experiences within these themes, and it is hoped that these findings could help inform developments in mental, physical, and social support during a benefit sanction.

2. Introduction

The poorest in society are often hit the hardest by recessions (Van Hal, 2015), and since 2010, the UK government under Conservative leadership has overseen an overarching policy of austerity (Lacbucci, 2010). While countries that adopted austerity measures, such as Greece, have seen a sharp increase in mental health issues, and suicides (Karinkolos et al, 2013), countries that have rejected austerity over the same period – like Iceland – did not (Corcoran et al, 2015).

In the UK, the link between poverty, deprivation, and poor mental health is well known (Knapp, 2012). Whilst an explicit link between changes and welfare and suicide remains controversial, the evidence is mounting in its favour (Mills, 2017). Barr and colleagues' work that found the Work Capability Assessment (WCA) appeared to result in six extra suicides per ten thousand undergoing the assessment (Barr et al, 2015). Barnes and colleagues also found among individuals admitted to A&E with self-harm injuries reported experiences framed by deprivation and trauma created by a sense of despair at their circumstances (2016). It can be assumed that the economic hardship brought on by austerity measures, usually on top of intergenerational poverty and area deprivation, merge into the 'final straw' to trigger further poor mental health – and more likely to impact greatest on those already dealing with mental health issues (Patrick, 2017).

Nearly half of all disability benefit claims in the UK are due to poor mental health (Banks et al, 2015). The notoriously dispassionate welfare system has come under intense public scrutiny for its impact on individuals experiencing long-term deprivation, physical and mental illness (Arni et al, 2013), who have been equally vilified and supported in the national media

(Runswick-Cole et al, 2015). One particular action used by the Department of Work and Pensions (DWP) to punish those judged to have infringed Jobcentre rules is a benefits sanction – a temporary suspension on regular benefits allowance from anywhere between 4 to 36 weeks, and has been applied for myriad superfluous reasons such as; not looking for work on Christmas Day, and having a heart attack during an assessment (Butler, 2016). Research has linked sanctions to sudden and severe mental health crisis, such as anxiety, depression, and suicide (McVeigh, 2016; Barr et al, 2015), and found the action to have little effect as a deterrent or evidence that suggests it is fit for purpose (National Audit Office, 2016).

Although mental health conditions differ vastly in impact, the nature of the conditions often take a heavy toll on the individual, and interferes with day-to-day life (Mashiach-Eizenberg et al, 2013). However, in-depth research into the impact of poor mental health while in the UK welfare system is limited, especially during a sanction period. Mental health is defined by the World Health Organization (WHO) as "*a state of well-being in which every individual realizes [their] potential, can cope with normal stresses, and work productively to make a contribution to [their] community*" (WHO, 2014). Research has found that a proportion of individuals with mental health difficulties make the choice to not seek help from formal services at all, or mix formal services with self-care behaviours (Oliver et al, 2005), which can include everything from support groups, exercise, and drug use (Patton et al, 2002).

2.1 Disability Welfare Reforms

Under the last coalition government, the welfare-to-work programme was rolled out across the UK in 2011 in order to address the country's apparent 'welfare dependence' (DWP,

2015), often seen by wider society as inherently problematic and a sign of 'broken Britain' (Slater, 2014). This programme was primarily the overhaul of assessment for those claiming Employment Support Allowance (ESA), or other incapacity benefit. Resting on the basis of assessment of an individual's functional capacity and abilities, rather than descriptions of disabilities or health conditions, those in receipt of ESA were reassessed. Under this new programme, individuals living with chronic health conditions, including complex mental health difficulties underwent the new WCA. The DWP then phased out the former Disability Living Allowance (DLA) to be replaced with Personal Independence Payment (PIP), a notorious non-means tested, two-tiered benefit comprised of a daily-living, and mobility component (Cross, 2013). Lastly, the DWP, under the Welfare Reform Act (2012), began the roll out of the controversial Universal Credit scheme in an attempt to streamline almost all existing benefits, while limiting the amount any one individual can claim (DWP, 2015).

However, it has been found that negative incentivisation of vulnerable individuals by switching to a smaller benefit with a higher compliancy rate – usually in the form of a benefits sanction – in the hopes of eventual employment, does not work (Arni et al, 2013). In fact, this move has proved to be extremely damaging to social, physical, and mental health of individuals (McCarthy et al, 2015; McNeil et al, 2017). Statistics released by the DWP reveal that over two thousand three hundred individuals died after failing their WCA between 2011 and 2014 alone (DWP, 2015). Further still, the DWP itself is investigating its own direct link in the suicide of over sixty individuals since 2012 (ONS, 2013), illustrating a worrying trend towards increased mortality in those being found fit for work after a WCA, and public outcry (Franklin, 2013; O'Hara, 2014).

2.1.1 Impact of Welfare Reforms

Individuals living with complex mental health difficulties constitute over forty percent of WCA attendees (DWP, 2015), with nearly fifty percent of these individuals having had an initial fit for work decision appealed and overturned, bringing into question the validity of these assessments (Shakespeare et al, 2017). Of those living with complex health needs, including mental health difficulties, nearly seventy-three thousand experienced a benefits sanction, with over five thousand experiencing a rolling sanction up to six months (Authority US, 2015), suggesting these processes do not take in to account sufficient information on impact of condition on daily living, nor consider the impacts of negative measures to force compliancy (Shakespeare et al, 2017). Benefit sanctions in particular have been shown to add unnecessary and unwarranted stress and financial hardship on those already vulnerable (Barnes et al, 2016; Garthwaite, 2014).

2.2 The Psychological Influence of Austerity

Although receiving little attention via the mainstream press, the link between wider austerity measures and deteriorating mental health of the populace is becoming startlingly clear (Corcoran et al, 2015). McKee and colleagues (2012) found that austerity measures implemented after the financial crisis led to a six-fold increase in suicides in European countries that adopted said measures, but stayed stable in those countries which did not adopt them (Branas et al, 2015; Haw et al, 2015). This supports previous research into the interpersonal theories of mental health, suicide in particular;

with societal stigma towards benefit claimants, and feelings of isolation and burden all increasing the risk of suicidal thoughts (van Orden et al, 2010; Mills, 2017). Furthermore, research has found that in industrial capitalist cities like Glasgow, depression is on the rise (Halpern, 2014).

Psychologist Oliver James highlighted this increase as taking place from the 1950s onwards, and made the point that as we as a society grew richer economically, we grew poorer emotionally (James, 1998). This is he argues, in part, down to the portrayal of the 'perfect life' and its portrayal on media outlets – and today on social media – something which is ultimately impossible to fulfil (De Choudhury, 2013). On the other hand, Martin-Carrasco and colleagues (2016) highlight the increasingly difficult living needs within such cities as a factor in spiralling poor mental health, such as: lack of meaningful employment (Karanikolos et al, 2016), personal debt (Richardson et al, 2013), and housing instability (Novoa et al, 2015), all of which can then be further exacerbated by a benefits sanction. With researchers such as Mattheys (2016) suggesting that the spiralling mental health difficulties of the populace, far from being influenced by the financial downturn itself, are in fact the product of the harsh realities of austerity measures, namely, the welfare-to-work programme and its series of compliancy measures (O'Hara, 2014; Patrick, 2017). This was further backed by Loopstra and colleagues' (2015) work, which found compliancy measures such as benefit sanctions put affected individuals at increased risk of destitution and associated poor mental health, with increasing numbers of individuals living with complex mental health difficulties having benefits sanctioned due to non-compliance, and highlighting the welfare system's apparent ignorance of influencing psychosocial factors on the claimant relationship (Patrick, 2016).

2.2.1 Consequences of Poverty & Deprivation in Glasgow

Social inequality, including poverty and deprivation, has been shown to have a detrimental effect on health (Rambotti, 2015), with a particularly baffling phenomenon affecting the area in which this research took place, known as The Glasgow Effect – referring to the unexplained poor life expectancy of Glasgow residents in comparison to the rest of the UK (Walsh et al, 2010). Research has found that lower income levels are often associated with poor health and shorter lifespan (Marmot et al, 2012); however the prevailing consensus among health epidemiologists is that poverty alone cannot account for the disparities found in Glasgow, as theorised more recently by Walsh and colleagues (2017). Strangely, equally deprived industrial areas in the UK, such as Liverpool, in fact have higher life expectancies, with even the wealthiest 10% of the Glasgow population having a lower life expectancy than their peers in other parts of the UK (McCartney et al, 2010).

However, Cowley and colleagues' (2016) recent research suggests that it is the coalescence of multiple stress-inducing factors that expose the Glaswegian population to the unusually high levels of stressors felt. Although low socioeconomic status can breed stress, certain 'Glaswegian' characteristics also add to the life-reducing toll; continued resistance to healthy lifestyle choices, especially amongst males (Sloan et al, 2010) as part of a 'macho' approach to health, have also been cited to contribute to the low life expectancy seen in Glasgow.

Furthermore, Whyte and colleagues (2010) found that health-related indicators of life expectancy, such as psychological morbidity, cancer deaths, chronic diseases, and inadequate diets seem to be pervasive across socio-economic groups in Glasgow. Biopsychosocial factors, such as environment, have also been cited as possible burdens contributing to the Glasgow effect (McCartney et al, 2011). Also the legacy of immigration

– descendants of Irish immigrants to Glasgow show an increase in premature mortality risk, even when those risk factors are controlled for (Abbots et al, 1998). It can be seen that there is no clear, simple, or singular factor ultimately responsible for the effect (Reid, 2009).

Cowley and colleagues (2016) conclude that the stress response, so integral to survival in the historical context, is now misplaced in modern first-world populations. The oftentimes chronic activation of that response to everyday events, such as money worries, social status, and health is thought to – in part – drive the Glasgow effect through the negative consequences of persistent overexposure to elevated stressors, which can also be seen to be present in other unequal societies (Kondo et al, 2009; Thornicroft et al, 1991) – which, coupled with negative health behaviours and choices embedded in cultural beliefs, conspire to the conditions seen in the Glasgow effect (Ganzel et al, 2010; Sheridan et al, 2013). This position has been further supported in recent work by Samuel and colleagues, who theorise poverty – which can breed feelings of shame and humiliation due to stigma (Hills, 2015) – caused by austerity measures can in turn lead to mental health difficulties due to worsening of social inequality (Bambra et al, 2015). With public opinion and rhetoric turning extremely negative towards those experiencing poverty and deprivation, mental health difficulties, or claiming benefits (Briant et al, 2011; Geigar et al, 2017), individuals facing these hardships are increasingly questioning their place in society.

2.3 Understanding Citizenship in Society

T. H. Marshall framed citizenship as condition, and as being part of a community (Marshall, 1950). An individual's sense of belonging, self-worth, and inclusion within their community, wider society, and nationally, is invariably tied to, and dependent on, their citizenship status (Lister, 2003; Dwyer, 2010). Whether this citizenship is viewed solely as a status that delivers a packet of rights and responsibilities, or as a set of demands that have to be carried out in a satisfactory way to be deemed 'engaged', the word focuses attention on inclusion and exclusion – on who is, and who isn't deemed a 'citizen' within a certain framework (Dwyer, 2010). Clarke and colleagues (2014) theorise that citizenship is not a static state for the individual; the boundaries often blur and shift, with those who experience their citizenship status as precarious, or find themselves treated as second-class citizens for various reasons (Dwyer, 2010). This is often related to the extent of their engagement and place in wider society – young, old, workers, or unemployed. A spectrum that the individual can move along depending on societal, community, and political norms, expectations, and demands placed on them as citizens of that nation (Lister, 2003). This gives a particular relevance to the exploration of how individuals respond to changes in their social security, personal lives, mental health, and entitlement over time – just a selection of a raft of changes that can impact on what it means to 'be a citizen'.

2.3.1 Conditional Citizenship

Recent welfare reforms and practices have been justified as part of a societal effort to support the 'social inclusion' of benefit recipients by encouraging individuals to foster a 'hard working ethic' – to become good, productive citizens (Levitas, 1998). This creates a particular lens in which to view benefits, sanctions, and mental health, and what it means to being a 'good social citizen'. Alongside this, it is also indispensable in exploring what rights, both social and personal, that being a citizen of a particular society provides. Whether or not citizenship within the UK today provides a 'modicum of economic welfare and security' (Marshall, 1950) or that, in entering the welfare system, this protection is taken away from who society views as bad citizens (Lister, 2003).

To explore this concept, T.H. Marshall's theory of social citizenship is particularly relevant. This classical, liberal egalitarian concept was developed by Marshall to emphasise the equality of all citizens (Bode, 2008). Marshall's theory charted the public emergence of the political, civil, and social rights of citizenship from the 18th to 20th centuries. Of particular interest is the conceptualisation of social citizenship, defined by Marshall as "the whole range [of social rights] from the right to a modicum of economic welfare and security, to the right to share to the full in the social heritage and to live the civilised life according to the standards prevailing in society" (Marshall, 1950). Although heated debate has existed since on the extent, interpretation, and reach of Marshall's social rights (White, 2003), agreement exists on their intrinsic value, with social citizenship having real value and significance for those living in poverty and deprivation (Dwyer, 2010). Furthermore, Marshall's theory frames how political, civil, and social rights are inevitably intertwined, to such an extent that the denial of one category impacts on the individual's capacity to exercise the others, described as the 'three-legged stool of citizenship' by Twine (Twine, 1994).

However, this concern with rights has led to criticisms over the individual's own responsibilities within the theory (Etzoni, 1995). Although not explicitly laid out, the theory emphasises the importance of paid employment, and the duty of individuals to live the life of a 'good citizen' through employment, and put their efforts into their work (Marshall, 1950). Combined with criticisms over neglect of women's rights, political in particular, as well as neglect of the issues of disability and gender, this had led to some stipulating that Marshall's theory of social citizenship was designed to focus on white, healthy, adult males (Delanty, 2000; Dwyer, 2010; Williams, 1992).

Nonetheless, Marshall's theory of social citizenship remains valuable in providing a framework that can be utilized to defend social welfare. By raising awareness of social citizenship, and calling on the state to provide some level of decommodified – upholding a socially acceptable standard of living independent of market participation (Epsing-Anderson, 1990) – support to those in need, this placed contractual onerous demands on the state. This provision of decommodified social security support by the state has been key since the post-war welfare effort, as well as elemental in conceptualising Marshall's theory of social rights. Although Marshall's ambiguous writing around the nature and extent of social rights limits the utility of his ideas, his framework's emphasis on social rights has resonance when exploring the nature and consequences of social welfare reform, and its impact on individuals. This is particularly useful when used to frame at the dominant narratives of recent governments views of out-of-work welfare, and claimant's own experiences.

2.3.2 Value of the 'Poor'

Marshall's framework highlights the extent to which fair social citizenship can be of value to those living in poverty, and deprivation, while indicating how these experiences can undermine that very same citizenship – particularly when inequality in status is present.

Living in poverty and deprivation inherently encroaches on citizenship, and all three categories in Marshall's framework are largely unrealised for these individuals (Lister, 1990; Vincent, 1990) – Vincent stipulates that a 'poor citizen is a contradiction in terms'.

However, there has been ongoing debate over what, if anything, social citizenship offers to the poorest in society. In moving towards a post-Marshallian framework for an inclusive social citizenship, researchers such as Gaventa (2016) have emphasised the importance of looking beyond access to right and resources, and asking questions around recognition, participation, respect, and giving a voice. While the consensus agrees that meaningful access to resources is vital to social citizenship (Earle, 2017), they also emphasise the individual's right to be treated with respect and dignity, and their needs and preferences acknowledged and recognised, as highlighted by Leisering and colleagues (2013). This is particularly pertinent to those living with poverty and deprivation in society, as it is their voices that are heard the least, ignored, or even silenced in a world in which political points-scoring often ignores ground-level impact (McKee, 2017; Gaventa, 2012; Tayler, 2014). The importance of securing equal access participation is a seemingly challenging objective in Western societies, in which the poorest typically find it difficult to participate (Fraser, 2003). For this right to participate to be exercised meaningfully, familial and community forms of action, as well as awareness of political decision-making, should be considered (McKee, 2017). Considering these points, it is then possible to extend Marshall's model to include the issues those on benefits and living with a mental health difficulty face, that of receiving respect, having their voices heard, and recognition of the facets unique to their daily living (Earle, 2017; Patrick, 2017). This, of course, is a demanding framework, but one in which individual lived experiences can be listened to and given the voice they deserve (Thill, 2015; McKee, 2017; Gaventa, 2016).

2.4 Austerity 'Ailments'

With a view towards providing an evidence-based framework in order to understand the impact austerity has on mental distress, the group Psychologists Against Austerity (PAA; now

Psychologists for Social Change) developed and conceptualised the five 'austerity ailments' (2015). These ailments consist of; humiliation and shame; fear and distrust; instability and insecurity; isolation and loneliness; and being trapped and powerless. PAA's briefing paper draws a direct link between austerity measures, such as the increase in benefit sanctions, and the rise of poor mental health. Experiencing any of the austerity ailments as defined by PAA has been shown to increase mental health problems (PAA, 2015). In further support, previous research has found that following a severe loss – such as long-term employment – more than trebles the risk of suffering, and being diagnosed with, clinical depression (Economou et al, 2013), which can in turn lead to entering the benefits system. In turn, the Sparticus Report (2012) discovered the experience of job loss and entering the benefits system as a 'shameful' experience. Coupled with Kim and colleagues' theory that traditionally, shame is the 'bedrock of all psychopathology' (2011), job insecurity and loss can be just as damaging to mental health. With feelings of entrapment building over a period of insecurity or loss, it has subsequently been found that this situation can nearly treble the chances of being diagnosed with anxiety, and depression (Gallie et al, 2017). Similarly, lower levels of trust also increase the chance of being diagnosed with depression by more than 50% (Piccoli et al, 2015). The five ailments conceptualised by PAA are indicators of wider and deeper-rooted problems in society (Slater, 2014), of poisoned-apple policies and politics (Arni et al, 2015; McNeil et al, 2017), of the weakness and degrading of social cohesion (McKee, 2017; Patrick, 2017), and the widening inequality gap in power and wealth (Rambotti, 2015). The key markers of a healthy and equal society that is cohesive with participatory citizens who are mentally well include; agency, security, connection, meaning, and trust, which previous research has shown to be absent at the moment (PAA, 2015; Patrick, 2017). Mental health, although falling within the individual's experience, is not just an individual issue. To create the healthy and resilient society envisioned by PAA, the entirety of social and economic conditions in which individuals live need to be changed (2015). These austerity ailments may provide a useful framework in helping conceptualise how we understand the materialisation of distress in this study's context of poverty, deprivation, and wider austerity.

2.4.1 Cuts & Self-Care

Under austerity, publicly-funded services for people living with complex mental health difficulties continue to experience considerable pressure, financially and otherwise (Karanikolos et al, 2013). With mental health budgets continuing to be cut, and mental health difficulties on the rise (Lee et al, 2017; Martin-Carrasco et al, 2016), individuals are being left without formal support. Alonso and colleagues (2004) found that only around a third of individuals with mental health difficulties seek help from formal services, with the further two thirds not engaging due to a number of impacting factors, including local provision (Andrews et al, 2000; Clement et al, 2015). Therefore, those out of formal services utilise a number of informal support factors, including family, friends, and health choices (Funk, 2016; Brown et al, 2014).

Family and friends have an intrinsic part to play in the support network of an individual struggling with complex mental health difficulties – if utilised properly. Findings from Pernice-Duca (2010) highlighted that individuals living with complex mental health difficulties did benefit from family support, but only on their terms. Similarly, Pitschel-Walz and colleagues (2015) found that family members, when educated on their member's specific mental health difficulty, improved recovery outlook, and provided a valuable source of support out with hospital stays. However, in a review of support effectiveness, Repper and colleagues (2011) found that family and friends were rated to provide less support than peer support workers who were also relative strangers, perhaps due to non-disclosure to family, cultural differences, or fear of stigma (Hasson-Ohayon et al, 2011; Abdullah et al, 2011; Pickett et al, 2010). Health behaviours and choices have long been known to be influenced by social standing and environment (Pickett et al, 2010; Ganzel et al, 2010; Sheridan et al, 2013; Cowley et al, 2016). However, how these are in turn used to help cope with mental health difficulties in time of stress is less well known. Findings by Jackson and colleagues (2009) underlined the often-ignored used of negative health behaviours – such as drink and drug use – to cope with stressful situations or poor mental health. This is also supported by findings from Cotti and colleagues (2015), who observed higher rates of negative health behaviours during times of heightened stress and worsening mental health, including; smoking, excessive alcohol consumption, illicit drug use, and drink-driving (PAA, 2015; Patrick, 2017).

2.5. Aims

Although previous research has looked into the experience of claiming benefits in disabled, as well as mental health populations, few have explored and investigated the specific impact of a benefit sanction on already poor mental health (Patrick, 2017). Therefore, the aims of this study are: to explore the unique experience of living in Glasgow during a benefit sanction; how do individuals with complex mental health difficulties look after themselves while claiming benefits; and what impact did the benefit sanction have on their physical, social, and mental well-being. The qualitative exploration of this gap in the research could provide new insights into the significant, unique, and distinctive experiences of the individuals in this situation, and could help influence future policy around welfare, and physical, mental, and social support.

3. Methodology

3.1 Overview

This qualitative research study explored how individuals who have experienced a benefits sanction manage the impact on their mental health, and self-care. This chapter describes the methodology employed in this study; defining theoretical position, participant selection, recruitment, data collection, data analysis, and ethical considerations, all within a reflexive framework.

3.2 Theoretical Position

3.2.1 Design

This study is important and timely, as the voices of individuals on benefits struggling with poor mental health are particularly hidden within the interdisciplinary research literature around out-of-work benefits, socioeconomic class, and mental health. I wanted the individuals taking part in this study to be able to get all the unique nuances of their lived experience across without being constrained by structured interviews or quantitative data collection. Influenced by my own epistemological and ontological position as a researcher, an individual, and as someone who has lived through similar experiences, this section provides a brief overview of the theoretical underpinnings that influenced the methodology of this research study.

3.2.2 The Theoretical Orientations of Interpretative
Phenomenological Analysis (IPA)

Interpretative Phenomenological Analysis' (IPA) primary goal is to explore how individuals make sense of their particular experiences, on the assumption that these individuals are 'self- interpreting beings' (Taylor, 1985), actively engaging in interpreting these events, objects, and other people in their lives. To explore this individual process, IPA draws on the fundamental, and long-standing principles of phenomenology, hermeneutics, and idiography (Smith et al, 2009).

Developed by Husserl, phenomenology, an eidetic method, is primarily concerned with understanding the way individuals perceive an experience in their own unique way. By using eidetic reductionism, researchers employing phenomenology try to understand the components of the situation that make it unique. Phenomenological-based studies, therefore, focus on how the individuals perceive and talk about the situation, rather than just the description of the situation according to wider categorical systems, and in doing so the researcher must put aside any preconceived notions to allow the individuals and sense- making of the situation speak for themselves (Creswell et al, 2017).

Husserl's work was developed further by Heidegger (1962) into existential philosophy and importantly, hermeneutics – from the Greek 'to make clear' (SEoP, 2017), and concerned with the ontological question of existence (Freeman, 2008). Consequently, in using IPA, researchers attempt to place themselves in their participants' shoes – while recognising this can only be done to a certain extent. Through this interpretative activity meaning is explored and interpreted by the researcher in a dynamic process in which the researcher influences extent of access, and depth of sense-making of the participants experiences. This analytical process within IPA is often described as a double hermeneutic, or duel interpretation, as participants make meaning of their experiences, in which the researcher then tries to decode that meaning to make sense of the participants' sense-making (Smith et al, 2008). This synthesis of ideas from both phenomenology and hermeneutics results in a descriptive but interpretative method which lets the participants and sense-making speak for themselves (Smith et al, 2009).

The last orientation of IPA is idiography, the in-depth analysis of single cases in order to examine the participants' individual and unique perspectives (Rolin, 2009). In contrast with nomothetic principles that underlines most empirical work in mental health, IPA relies on idiography, shifting focus to the particular rather than the universal (Smith et al, 1995). As such, specific statements can be made due to this detailed exploration case by case by the researcher, resulting in important themes being generated and exemplified with samples of individual data which can then be compared and contrasted (Karp, 2013). This idiographic obligation is unusual, even among other qualitative methodologies, making it the perfect choice to explore the lived experiences of poor mental health in the context of a benefits sanction.

3.3 Recruitment

The initial criteria were to include one to ten participants, of any gender, above eighteen years of age, who identifies, or is diagnosed with, a mental health condition, has experienced a benefits sanction, and is resident in Glasgow. The potential difficulties in accessing this hard-to-reach group informed the decision to include these criteria, as well as informing my recruitment methods. Convenience sampling was used to recruit participants due to the nature of the study, and I had previous contacts with several third sector groups, and premises who could display my recruitment poster (appendix A), or inform their clients and service-users of my study. The general nature of the participant group I was looking to recruit made them a hard-to-reach group with the potential for vulnerability at a time of potential crisis. They would also not necessarily have access to mobile phones, computers, or the internet in order to see recruitment advertisements for this study online. This involved a focus on word-of-mouth, and 'analogue' recruitment measures involving areas traditionally utilised by individuals meeting the criteria, including libraries, foodbanks, community hubs and noticeboards, housing associations, informal support groups, and local advocates and campaigning groups. I approached several groups to display my recruitment poster, and inform service-users of this study, including: eight community integration networks, five community hubs (including Money Matters and Citizens Advice Bureau), fifteen mental health support groups, social enterprises, and charities operating locally, all thirty-two public libraries in Glasgow, twenty-seven community halls, ninety-three housing associations, seven local foodbanks, and fourteen online campaigning and advocacy groups, as well as traditional online methods such as placing an advert on Gumtree, Facebook, and Twitter. The recruitment materials also made their own way onto several platforms by other means, including Reddit (a photo was taken of the flyer and posted on the site), supermarket noticeboards (flyers had been posted), and brought to the attention of local support groups I had not personally contacted, but by the facilitators who had seen my flyers elsewhere.

3.3.1 Participant Selection

Six males and one female were recruited via personal contacts, third-sector support services, and other methods described above. One individual was removed from the study due to unacceptable behaviour towards the researcher, two individuals requested to be withdrawn from the study after their interviews, and one further individual could not be contacted to arrange an interview after an initial expression of interest. As such, the final sample of three participants was included in this study. Smith and colleagues (2013) recommend a sample size of between one and six participants for a master's project of this size utilising IPA, and this was achieved. Participant anonymity is protected via the use of pseudonyms, and mental and physical health conditions shared via participant requests.

Michelle K Jamieson

Table 1: Sample Characteristics					
Participant	**Age**	**Gender**	**No. of Benefit Sanctions**	**Mental Health Condition(s)**	**Other Conditions**
William	37	Male	2	Mania, Psychosis	ADHD, Dyspraxia, Dyslexia, Deaf
Robert	37	Male	2	Depression, Anxiety	Addiction, eye injury
Keith[1]	[R.]	Male	[Redacted]	[Redacted]	[Redacted]
Aaron	51	Male	2	PTSD, Social Anxiety, OCD	Head Injury, Misc. physical injuries
Peter[2]	[R]	Male	[Redacted]	[Redacted]	[Redacted]
Stephanie[3]	[R]	Female	[Redacted]	[Redacted]	[Redacted]
Age Range:					**37-51**
Scottish: English: Irish: Welsh: Other:					3(6): 0:0:0:0
[1] = Withdrawn from study due to assault. [2] = Withdrawn from study at request of participant. [3] = Data withdrawn at request of the participant.					

3.4 Data Collection

The qualitative approach adopted required a consideration of how best to explore and give a voice to the participants' sense-making of their experiences in a way that was meaningful to them.

Therefore, it was important to find a method of data collection that would provide space for the participants to discuss individual experiences that were important to them within the focus of poor mental health, benefit sanctions, and self-care. This section outlines the interview schedule, interview process and challenges faced.

3.4.1 Interview Schedule

Formulating an interview schedule within the IPA methodology involves promoting an open and inductive approach to the data collection, as well as the analysis. As IPA emphasises the idiographic exploration of experiences, it aims at generating rich and detailed descriptions of their sense-making of the situation under investigation (Pietkiewicz et al, 2014). Its call for in-depth exploration calls for open, overarching research questions, which in this study were;

1. What is the lived experience of living on benefits with a mental health issue in Glasgow?
2. What measures, formal or informal, do they take to manage their mental health?
3. What effect did benefits sanctions have on their mental health?

To explore these fully, while allowing the nuanced voice of experience unique to each participant, the interview schedule was designed to be a quite 'loose' semi-structured approach (appendix B). However, it did touch upon all relevant themes prominent in the study; experiences of poor mental health, the impact of benefits sanctioning, and self-care – all within the wider context of austerity in Scottish society.

3.4.2 Procedure

All of the interviews took place in a semi-pubic place in which the participants felt comfortable, including; a branch of a popular coffee chain in Glasgow city centre, a popular branch of a well-known fast food chain, and a public library in Glasgow. Interviews lasted between one hour and ten minutes and one hour and forty-five minutes, with only three of the six being used in analysis.

An informal screening process was used before the interview then began to ascertain whether participants were well enough, physically and mentally, at that particular time to carry out the interview; all agreed that they were. Interviews were headed by an explanation of the research (appendix C), and participants were given time to read through the information sheet and ask any questions before starting. The consent form (appendix D) was walked through and signed by both participants and researcher once comfortable. It was anticipated that deeply personal issues such as physical and mental trauma, loss, and generally other issues unique to a potentially vulnerable participant might be raised in the interviews. As such. strategies to minimise risk and distress were put in place, and involved assuring the participants that although these topics may come up in the interview, they were free to pause, take a break, move to another question, or stop the interview all together.

Interviewer safeguarding measures were also put in place. Five of the six interviews then proceeded without incident; the third interview, however, has been withdrawn from this research study due to the participant's actions.

The interviews were audio recorded on a Dictaphone recorder to ensure accuracy, and informal notes were also taken throughout. All interviews were relaxed, and the choice of venue – all being semi-public places with a modicum of privacy but busy enough not to be overheard – gave the participants confidence and control to go into what they wanted. In a few cases, after the interviews has officially ended, and the debrief was done, the participant and I spent some time finishing food or drink and conversing informally. All participants were happy with how the interview went, and a few stated it was good to have someone to talk so openly about it. A few of the participants spoke about other issues once the interview and recording had ended. These were private insights into their lives which I was privileged to hear, and was happy to have built some trust and rapport with them in that short time. In regards to the research, these have also added further depth to the coding, analysis, and findings somewhat unconsciously. Respecting these insights is an important ethical decision for me as a researcher, and although officially not in the analysis helps further understanding of the context, challenges, and opportunities participants have had in terms going through life dealing with seriously poor mental health while dealing with the impact of austerity.

3.4.3 Challenges

The interviews were not without their challenges, but for the majority of interviews these related to time, and keeping participants relatively on track, although deviations into their own unique epistemological experiences is a welcome and intrinsic part of the IPA process. One interview, however, was deeply challenging on a personal and professional level, and due to behaviour resulting in sexual harassment of the researcher on the day, and continuing over the period of a week, the decision was made to remove interview three from this study all together.

3.5 Data Analysis

A loose theoretical framework was used to steer and help contextualise the analysis, and consists of the fundamental theories that emerged from the literature review;

1. T.H. Marshall's Theory of Citizenship
2. Austerity Ailments & Self-Care

3.5.1 Transcription

IPA requires a verbatim record of the event in which data collection took place. As analysis in IPA aims to interpret and understand the content of that particular participants' account, it does not require an overly detailed transcription of the prosodic elements of the recorded interviews; however, some were still included here. It is important to recognise the power of non-verbal interactions in contextualising the interview – such as in this case – and can even be considered a form of interpretative activity in itself (Smith et al, 2009). IPA does require,

however, a semantic transcription, usually conventionally spelt. However, 'non-conventional' words or phrases – such as might appear in regional dialects or slang, can also be included as they too enrich the analysis (Smith et al, 2009). The temporality and historicity of the participants' experience is considered central to IPA's idiographic investigative commitment in context (Reid et al, 2005). Analysis proceeded on a case-by-case basis (Smith et al, 2008).

3.5.2 Coding

Interpretative Phenomenological Analysis (Smith et al, 2009) was used to examine the participants' experiential accounts (Eatough et al, 2006) and identify salient themes in and across cases. Table 2, adapted from Smith and colleagues (Smith et al, 2009; 2010), sets out the steps followed in coding.

Management of coding was done through basic software: Microsoft Word, and by hand. SuperOrdinate and SubOrdinate themes were uncovered from repeated readings of the transcripts and in and across case codes (appendix E).

Table 2: Levels of Interpretative Phenomenological Analysis (adapted from Smith et al, 2009; Smith, Flowers & Larkin, 2010)	
Level of analysis	**Description**
Familiarisation	Reading and rereading to gain familiarity with the transcript.
Gaining insight	Highlighting significant excerpts.
Categorisation	Grouping of excerpts in each transcript.
Pattern recognition	Identifying themes across cases.
Interpretation	The researcher combines accounts and prepares an interpretation.
Discussion	Production of theoretical explanations.

3.6 Ethical Considerations

Ethical approval for this study was sought and approved by the College of Social & Political Sciences Ethics Committee, with interviews taking place at a site chosen by the participants.

3.6.1 Researcher Safety

The 'Code of Safety for Social Researchers' published by the Social Research Association (2006) was utilised to assess and minimise risks to both myself and participants during this study. For example, I let a family member know where and when I was conducting an interview, I carried my fully charged mobile phone, and emergency cash for travel if I needed to leave a situation suddenly.

3.6.2 Potential for Participant Distress

Given the sensitive and emotive nature of the topic, the researcher was aware that some participants may become upset during the interview. The voluntary nature of participation was emphasised at all times, so only individuals who chose to be involved were. Participants chose a venue in which they would be comfortable, and were assured that they did not have to answer any questions they were unwilling to, and that they could take a break from interview if necessary; however, none of the participants required this.

Attention was given to the participants' opinion about the interview after its end. All felt comfortable discussing their experiences and several participants reported that they derived a cathartic experience from their participation. Following each interview, participants were provided with a list of contacts for further support.

4. Findings

4.1 Overview

This qualitative aimed to study and explore how individuals living in Glasgow and experiencing a benefits sanction manage the impact on their mental health, and self-care choices. The results of this research are framed by T.H. Marshall's Theory of Citizenship (1950) and Psychologists Against Austerity's Austerity Ailments (2015).

4.2 Results

Three superordinate themes, and nine interrelated subthemes emerged from the analysis and are summarised in Table 3.

The themes identified and summarised essentially represent how the individual participants made sense of, and understood, the impact of their benefit sanction(s) on their mental health and well-being in particular. Quotations from the participants have been used to illustrate first- hand the themes and ground them within their unique lived experiences. In cases where subthemes presented differently to others, the divergent experiences are also discussed.

Super-Ordinate Themes	Sub-Ordinate Themes		
Table 3: Super- & Sub- Ordinate Themes			
Participants	**William**	**Robert**	**Aaron**
Life Lived in Shades of Grey	*"The lower echelons of society seem to be getting ground down"*: Punished for Being		
	"You can't just put people into the mad, bad, or sad box, you know": Tick-Box Culture		
	"My life was already going downhill anyway. I thought, 'I'm fucked', man a horrible existence": The Downward Spiral		
Good Citizen, Bad Citizen	*"The most vulnerable. The benefits claiming stuff, you've already got that label from the get go"*: Scrounger Stigma		
	"They need to see that, my drive, or what am I? Worthless": A Balancing Act		
	"You certainly can't live on it, d'you know what I mean? You're stuck, can survive and that's barely it": Survival & Costing the System		
Helping Hands	*"Valium was the answer, cannabis was the answer, drink was the answer"*: Self-Medicating		
	"Ehm... I'm a new man. Albeit imposed, but, hey ho!": Positive Change		
	"Knowing there's something...That's a better way. When I was very, very bad, I didn't think I had one, a destiny, so": Looking to the Future		

4.2.1 Life Lived in Shades of Grey

The first, and perhaps most overarching, superordinate theme to be identified encapsulates how the participants made sense of the impact their underlying mental, physical, and social issues had on their lives, as well as their treatment at the hands of the DWP, other official agencies, and members of the public, of a life lived out with black and white. Three subordinate themes emerged from the participant accounts: 1. Punished for being in the position where they need to turn to the government for help, 2. Encountering and having their unique difficulties forced into black and white tick boxes, and, 3. The downward spiral of physical, social, and especially mental health experienced once placed within the benefits sanctioning system.

4.2.1(a). "The lower echelons of society seem to be getting ground down": Punished for Being

All three participants expressed the view that the DWP, through the means of a benefit sanction, and wider society as a whole were almost punishing them for the misfortune of their situation, the control of which was often out of their hands. Robert especially expressed this view as one he had noticed throughout his life, but especially during the sanction period. His struggles with alcohol and drug addiction had, in his view, led to a lot of people looking down on him as unworthy of help, doomed to fail, and as a burden on society as he put nothing back in. Robert disclosed some family abuse, with the view that he was worthless starting from childhood and his alcoholic father. This view of himself could have been reinforced by society's wider views towards addiction and benefit claimants. Robert describes how, no matter what he done, he was written off under these views:

"See the thing is- feeling helpless about it, and not realising you need help, d'you know what I mean? Not being able to do, or ask. Who am I to them [society]? Who are we? I mean who are we to do anything about it? D'you know what I mean? I mean, who am I?" (Robert)

Robert conveys an overwhelming sense of feeling trapped and ashamed by his situation, and by the belief that society does not want to help him due to his perceived worthlessness and being able to meaningfully provide. These thoughts are so strong for Robert that he even questions the value of asking for help, or changing, when he is considered such a small and insignificant part of the bigger picture.

Aaron describes his absolute incredulity at the DWP's apparent disregard for the nuances in everyday life, especially when living with complex and enduring physical, and mental health difficulties. To Aaron, this strengthens his opinion around society's disregard for those claiming benefits as undeserving of help, or empathy:

"Halfway up the road I realise I've forgotten my tablets- So... Phones them, but of course they don't answer their phones. So, it goes to someone, it was India I think I got, I say, 'Tell them I'm going to be late', 'Yes, we'll tell them in two days'... No! [laughs]. No, no, no. So, I go back, get the tablets, make my way back down for the nine o'clock appointment, and it's twelve minutes past. Well, they said, 'You're sanctioned again'. I said, no, no, no. There's no point in trying to explain to them, they don't understand... life!" (Aaron)

Aaron draws attention to the surreal and burdensome way in which the system works, and the barriers even a simple action can throw up when trying to communicate with the DWP regarding benefits. His quotation illustrates the lack of insight the system has into the everyday challenges he can face through personal difficulties they are aware off. Aaron's anger and frustration is clearly evident as he tried to comply with the rules while the system continues to hobble him.

William's views were set against a background of relative wealth, being from a middle-class background, and noticing a difference in societal views, reactions, and opinions once his outward appearance and actions changed due to the onset of his complex mental health difficulties, which were further compounded by the pressures of a benefit sanction.

"They pulled us over and literally went, 'we need to talk to him'... And everyone was- cause generally you're dressed like a tramp. they pull me over, because of my issues. I take real offense to it! Then, of course all I'm getting is 'oh, you've got nothing to hide', so it shouldn't really bother that they want to strip you and stuff. It does bother me! Because I haven't actually done anything!" (William)

William's direct and angry approach suggest he believes he would be treated differently if he even dressed differently in certain situations. He also expressed disgust and, at times, surprise at the way he has been treated during his low period. He describes being extremely hurt and irritated by this treatment for the way he looks during a particularly dark time in his mental health, and was able to recognise this treatment in part due to his outward stereotypical appearance, which can be considered psychologically damaging at a time of isolation and fear bred due to insecurity.

4.2.1(b). "You can't just put people into the mad, bad, or sad box, you know": Tick- Box Culture

Two participants in particular expressed the knowledge of the existence, negative impact, and hardship brought on by the use of a 'tick-box culture', especially within the DWP, but also evident in society as a whole. Both conveyed the damage of this is reducing their suffering and larger nuances of life into black and white. William had a lot of experience of this, both when dealing with the DWP and also with the medical profession, as he had also been through the PIP process. He had experienced a particularly sudden and distressing onset of complex mental health difficulties, and took exception to the role GPs and psychiatrists in particular have in relation to the benefits process, and being, as he saw it, implicit in reducing his distress to a line on a form and branding him as 'abnormal':

> *"They just look at it by putting us in these little boxes. So, does society though! Uses these little boxes. Why do you need to get a diagnosis? Why? I just am who I am!" (William)*

The words and tone used convey the resentment William has for the way he has been treated. He resents being pigeonholed under a diagnosis, and having all subsequent behaviour put down to this. He in fact rejects his diagnosis – although due to it he is awarded PIP – and through this seems to take back some control of his rapidly spiralling situation. Aaron had experienced long-term physical, and in particular mental health, difficulties due to an earlier attack, which led to his situation and subsequent interaction with the DWP rapidly going downhill. The inflexibility of the system, and its apparent need for standardisable situations, have been particularly difficult for Aaron to work around while also dealing with complex mental health issues that he is still coming to terms with:

> *"It's not my fault the system doesn't work, and there's no flexibility, no ehm... you know, the world is not black and white! It isn't! But they- they do seem to think that!" (Aaron)*

Their need to fit everyone into a tick-box does not take into account the impact of complex mental health difficulties on everyday life. Aaron is incensed, as were it just for common sense and understanding, he would not have been sanctioned and faced the negative impacts on his already difficult situation. His incredulity also stems from the belief that the system cannot believe they can standardise life, and it is this system and lack of flexibility that led many to be sanctioned when not needed.

4.2.1(c). "My life was already going downhill anyway. I thought, 'I'm fucked', man a horrible existence": The Downward Spiral

Two participants expressed powerful insight into the moment they realised their mental, physical, and social health situations were in freefall, and if not rectified soon, would lead to a tragic and irreversible event. This downward spiral was deeply rooted in adversity, stigma – both external and internal – marginalisation and isolation, and lack of help available to them at the time, having a profoundly adverse effect on an already difficult situation. Robert especially had insight into this situation. Having developed severe depression and anxiety while dealing with long-term addiction, childhood trauma, and homelessness, he referenced his sanction period as the event that was both his lowest, and his revelation for what his life was:

"It's fucking frightening man... my mental health was rock-bottom. I mean, I've been in children's homes, young offenders, rehabs, detox, you name it man, I've not missed it! For them to go like that, right, boom! Sanctioned, man. You're like that to yourself, 'Right, where do I go from here?' Where do I go from here? (Robert)

Robert projected and externalised his beliefs and feelings around his situation during the majority of the interview, giving rise to the possibility that in framing his distress as suffered by others, it then validates his own, circumventing his belief that society views him as worthless for his situation. His anger stems from the apparent apathy of services and wider society towards their most vulnerable in times of severe distress. Similarity, Aaron also had a crystallised moment of realisation around his mental health in particular, and how he would end up if he didn't try to stop the freefall of his situation:

"When I was very, very ill... I didn't think I had a destiny, a future. I just thought, 'No'. The darkest days I either thought I'd kill myself, or I would just become... a vegetable, for want of a better word. I'd just sit watching Jeremy Kyle and drinking vodka all day. And that'd be my fate." (Aaron)

This quotation particularly captures Aaron's resignation over his situation in that moment. It illustrates his complete lack of control over the overwhelmingly impacting factor, the benefit sanction, his mental and physical fatigue and overall, his complete isolation from any help, and abandonment as a 'bad citizen'. His situation in particular was also framed by feeling trapped and seeing only one way out, and instability, causing the downward spiral in a man used to structure.

4.2.2 Good Citizen, Bad Citizen

The second superordinate theme characterises the psychological and physical processes in which the participants navigated their personal experiences of internal and external stigma, judgement and abonnement by society and the everyday practicalities of living with poor complex mental health difficulties during their sanction period. Three interrelated subthemes emerged reflective of this stage in their journey: 1. Dealing with wider societal views around claiming benefits and being sanctioned, or scrounger stigma, 2. The unique balancing act of being seen to be giving back to society, to be 'good', when trying to cope with the inherent 'badness' of mental health difficulties and their previewed burden on society, 3. The practicalities of physical and mental survival during the sanction period while dealing with the lowest point in their mental health, and guilt over burdening the larger system.

4.2.2(a). "The most vulnerable. The benefits claiming stuff, you've already got that label from the get go": Scrounger Stigma

Insidious thoughts, views, and actions around claiming benefits, and being sanctioned in particular were universal across all three participant accounts. This was experienced on a personal, and wider societal level, and also seemed to be internalised in one case. Robert in particular struggled with internalised stigma while also dealing with external stigma:

"You're already vulnerable... You've already got that stigma... eh label. You go into the Job Centre as it is, and for them to go- and especially their attitude towards us as well at that time- just sanctioning man! I mean, I was like- 'no way man!' Can you not just- you just need to have a wee bit of empathy, man- a wee bit of understanding!" (Robert)

This quotation illustrates Robert's view of his distress – albeit externalised, as he often portrayed his thoughts and feelings. Wider societal views around addiction and claiming benefits have perhaps internalised in Robert, and along with deep-rooted feelings of unworthiness have developed an almost self-fulfilling vicious prophesy of fitting society's views and being deserving of his situation. Only on looking back could he see he was deserving of compassion and help. William's account again carried notes of surprise over his treatment, due to not encountering it from a young age, like Robert. His particular view revolves around the role of psychiatric medication and 'curing' mental health difficulties in order to transition from benefit claimant and scrounger to a productive member of society:

"What's good for the person, what's good for society? It never matches, it's always what's good for society. Keep people medicated, keep them down. So, you can be shown to be 'good'. So, when you come off your medication, or have a bad time, you're somehow shit." (William)

In William's eyes, this transition, however desperately pushed by the DWP and psychiatry, could never be beneficial for the individual. The view that to be a good, productive member of society, off benefits and in work, means to be mentally well, and if taking medication achieves this, then in society's eyes this should be done. For William, this means giving up a large part of himself. He is comfortable with his, at times, poor mental health; for him the view that he is somehow a 'bad citizen' for refusing the notation of complete recovery is more far more damaging than the immediate scrounger stigma attached to claiming and a sanction. For Aaron, he is incredulous that this stigma persists, especially in the DWP itself, but realises it serves a purpose – to shame people off benefits:

"I'm told me that the staff all get warned... that they better start sanctioning people. They need to bring the numbers down, and it looks good when the bosses have a look, 'Oh well done!', slackers! Cut them down, all of that." (Aaron)

This institutionalised attitudes towards benefit claimants, and those sanctioned in particular strikes Aaron as serving the purpose of purely saving money. The fact that these attitudes have seeped out into wider society only helps their cause, further increasing feelings of humiliation and shame over a situation largely out of his hands.

4.2.2(b). "They need to see that, my drive, or what am I? Worthless": A Balancing Act

Robert in particular expressed the need to show he was now a 'good', productive member of society in contrast to his previous behaviour fitting stereotypical views of a benefits claimant struggling with addiction and poor mental health difficulties. He describes how his thinking around his self-worth, behaviour, and views changed towards the DWP, and his placed in society once some help had begun to trickle in:

"I learnt a lot of stuff in the rehab man, and how not to get annoyed and all that, how to deal with official bodies if you like. How to be proactive over the phone, be assertive in person, and not be passive-aggressive, good. I learned all that. Just because you're not in any sort of recovery or... that shouldn't be a reason as to why the way they are, know what I mean?" (Robert)

Robert's sense of self-worth and place in society seems firmly entwined with his behaviour and views and his personal recovery journey, and those expressed by others. When struggling with addiction and poor mental health, he very much considered himself a 'bad citizen', worthless, and not surprised at his situation. Now, looking back and considering himself successfully 'recovered', considers himself a 'good citizen', worthy of help, and a place in society as a productive member. Having come through it, it is evident throughout his interview that these insidious negative attitudes and stigma only serve to keep benefit claimants, particularly those under sanction, down.

4.2.2(c). "You certainly can't live on it, d'you know what I mean? You're stuck, can survive and that's barely it": Survival & Costing the System

Two participants, Robert and Aaron in particular, referenced living as surviving during their sanction period, as a half-life, and the negative impact effects in fact costing the system more than the sanction sought to save:

"The lengths I had to go to man to... just to survive. I mean you're looking down at even just the basics man, stealing bread, milk. But... and then- see after a while man, after the ways and means man, ran out... I was just isolated. That was all I done, just sit in the house, see. In the dark- I didn't even know if it was fucking night or day man, it didn't fucking matter anymore." (Robert)

Robert in particular felt very strongly on just how much of a damaging effect the benefit sanction had on him, alongside his addiction issues and mental health difficulties. At several points, he used the word 'animal' to describe what his behaviour made him feel like, just in order to survive. Criminal activity which at the beginning purely fuelled an addiction gradually transitioned towards stealing basics such as bread in order to eat, until even that is pushed to the background by the negative effects on his mental health. Aaron in particular is struck by just how much his downward spiral brought on by his benefit sanction cost the NHS and similar systems:

"Routine and structure, they're taking it away. Imagine how much money they're costing the NHS? My psychiatrist, she works within the NHS as a... a psychiatrist, they don't come cheap! You know, they do not come cheap! Ehm... so all this is... for the sake, of what? Because the DWP don't have any proper... system, because there's no flexibility in the system? No accountability, its- it's a horrible thing. How one decision can have such a massive... yeah." (Aaron)

This quote encapsulates his underlying anger, and resignation at the system itself. Aaron considers it not fit for purpose, and in fact voices the opinion that it only perpetuates itself in costing other linked systems more due to negative impact, and feeding the same people back into the benefits system. For Aaron, this same system reduces living down to pure survival, which in turn feeds into the participants' downward spiral mental health wise.

4.2.3 Helping Hands

The third superordinate theme to emerge frames the participants' experiences and choices around mental health self-care in particular, and the impact this had on their situations. The three subthemes that emerged in turn illustrate the paradoxical nature of choice and impact at times for the individual participants, but also their similarities in regards to coping with a dire situation: 1. Self-medicating as a form of self-care in light of apathetic services, 2. Seeing a positive change in themselves and their situation, and, 3. Being able to see their future.

4.2.3(a). "Valium was the answer, cannabis was the answer, drink was the answer": Self-Medicating

All three participants referenced using alcohol and non-prescribed drugs as a way to cope, and help them through their difficult sanction period, and also to help in coping with increasingly spiralling and complex mental health difficulties. William on the other hand also references use of prescribed psychiatric medication recreationally:

> *"Eh, Citalopram, Tramadol, Amitriptyline. Eh, beta-blockers, Propranolol. Which I used to take for fun! Not for its actual purpose, fuck that! Never [laughs]." (William)*

This is surprising considering William's aversion to prescribed psychiatric drugs as a form of coercion and control by the wider system, and the DWP in particular. However, due to lack of control over the benefit sanction, and the wider situation as a whole, turning the use of psychiatric drugs on its head as a way to introduce self-care, perhaps some control was regained. His overall tone, demeanour and use of words point towards acceptance of this behaviour, which led onto other self-care behaviours. Aaron references a heavy use of alcohol in particular, which only came around once his mental health had spiralled and his situation became dire due to the benefit sanction:

> *"Then I realised that it was just getting absolutely crazy-pardon the pun! But it was just mad, mad, mad. Ehm... by self-medicating by drinking vodka, like water, you know. Obviously, I had my meds, and then CBT, so..." (Aaron)*

For Aaron, drinking alcohol had its place in his self-care regime at the beginning. Through realising this use could not go on, he then took steps to get further help that worked for him. In his case psychiatric medication proved helpful in the beginning, and then a course of CBT also helped through providing a new structure, which in turned resulted in healthier physical and mental health choices and regaining a measure of control in order to cope with the benefit sanction. Robert made extensive use of alcohol and drugs as a self-care mechanism for not only his spiralling mental health, but also during his benefit sanction period, which he now recognises as a long-standing problem with addiction:

> *"I committed more crimes to get more- Valium was the answer, cannabis was the answer, drink was the answer. So, see if-man, that's what it comes back to- see for that two hundred quid, or whatever it was, I've cost the system an absolute fortune! Going in and taking convulsions man, full of Valium and drink- going into A&E, going to eh- police stations and that, going through the courts." (Robert)*

For Robert, this quote illustrates his ambivalence towards his extreme alcohol and drug use at the time, so much so that he is ending up in A&E. For him, the choice to take those drugs represented some semblance of control over the situation, while also providing him with a release from the fear and instability inherent during the sanction period. Only once coming through rehab and considering himself physically and mentally recovered can he look back, almost detached, and see the self-medicating behaviours as also detrimental to his already complex mental health difficulties at the time of the sanction.

4.2.3(b). "Ehm... I'm a new man. Albeit imposed, but, hey ho!": Positive Change

Robert and Aaron in particular reference a definite turn towards positive change in their lives, physical and mental health, living situation, facilitated through considered self-care choices and behaviours:

> *"Eh... keeping mentally active. I study, disciplined study. Ehm... exercise, and eh... eating well. Again, all this comes from... a lot of it is CBT stuff. I never used to do all these things! I was quite happy doing my job, getting my wages, you know- eating junk, going to the pub, da de da de dah."*
> *(Aaron)*

Although Aaron recognises the benefit taking these healthier choices has had on his physical and mental health, as well as giving back some control over the situation and providing a structure he can work and live within, he also recognises that it took a deteriorating situation to get to this stage. A situation that should never have happened in the first place.

Robert, similarly, saw a much more positive change in his physical and mental health and subsequent self-care choices after successfully completing a detox programme:

> *"It's just a fucking shame, because it wasn't until I started getting into recovery that... all the benefit stuff, and all that started taking care of itself. And that's a shame man, because... [laughs]. What? You need to go into fucking recovery man-some detox centre to start getting your life together before... things start to get sorted? That's not an option for everybody."*
> *(Robert)*

Robert admits that he feels incredibly lucky to have had the chance to enter a detox programme for his addiction that also offered help for his complex mental health difficulties as well. Without this chance, he admits to seeing himself stuck in the same vicious cycle of negative self-care choices and behaviour as behaviour, which was only made worse by the sanction. His anger and resentment of the long-running apathy from services during the sanction period at his situation and cries for help is evident throughout. However, now he considers himself in a much better place, physically, mentally, and socially, he tries to give back through advocacy, further enforcing his new positive beliefs around his worthiness as a good citizen who makes positive choices.

4.2.3(c). "Knowing there's something... That's a better way. When I was very, very bad, I didn't think I had one, a destiny, so": Looking to the Future

All three participants ended on a happier note by outlining and envisioning their futures beyond the worst of their sanction periods. All expressed surprise at being able to do this, as the situation had led to dark thoughts and actions during their lowest points. For Aaron, being able to look to his future signals his hard work in improving his mental health during one of the most difficult situations in his life is paying off:

"When I was very, very ill... I didn't think I had a destiny, a future, I just thought, 'No'. This is, either... in the darkest days I either thought I'd kill myself, or... I would just become... a vegetable, for want of a better word. I'd just sit watching Jeremy Kyle and drinking vodka all day. And that'd be my fate [sighs]. So... that's what I did, give myself a... a- something to aspire to, what's keeping me- Now I see a future, and that's good." (Aaron)

This quote encapsulates the broad spectrum of feeling portrayed by Aaron in this moment. For him to have come such a way in his thinking represents regaining of control and stability over his situation, in spite of his sanction still ongoing at time of the interview. For Robert, successfully completing a detox programme and improving his mental health difficulties via positive self-care choices enabled him to look at his sanction situation, and what he could do to take back some control:

"I'm just glad- that's one of the reasons I'm going to college man, so I don't need to- 'Cause I'll not be on this ESA for much longer man. I don't expect to be, and I don't want to be! Know what I mean? I'm not wanting- I don't want to fiddle the system anymore. Eh, but I'll deal with it just now until I go to college, d'you know what I mean? Basically, one of the main reasons I want to go to college- I want to learn about health and social care, help others" (Robert)

In realising he can have a future, and beyond by his recent success in detox, and fulfilling experiences as an advocate, he has begun to look towards his future with long-term goals. Through attending college, he envisions being able to help those in similar situations, as well as improving his own views on his own self-worth by lifting himself out of the scrounger and addict stereotypes placed on him by wider societal views. Switching, in society's eyes, from a 'bad' citizen and apparent burden on the system to a 'good' citizen who has successfully recovered physically and mentally, makes good choices and meaningfully contributes to society, has been a personal goal evident throughout Robert's narrative. William, on the other hand, has seen his future and giving back to society via setting up his own business, being his own boss, and showing he could embody the traditional 'good citizen', while also providing opportunities for others going through what he had with his mental health, and the belief that as he's grown older, his mental health difficulties have begun to resolve as he makes more decisions based on his own needs:

"I think it's 'cause I'm getting older, it's getting slightly better. I think it's kinda- I've got- I think it kinda affects you quite young, kind of- yeah early thirties, I kinda feel like coming out the end of... kind of growing out of it almost." (William)

For William, it was evident throughout that he associated his rapid mental health decline and sanction period as two separate entities almost unrelated to one another, as just another thing to deal with. In framing his mental health as a purely biological illness that crops up or gets worse at times of stress enabled him to gain some semblance of control over a rapidly deteriorating physical, mental, and social situation, which in turn enabled him to take steps meaningful to him. William's views throughout are in stark contrast to Robert and Aaron's, in which they very much place their poor mental health as firmly intertwined with their social situation and standing.

5. Discussion

5.1 Overview

This study explored the lived experience of living in Glasgow with complex mental health difficulties at the time of a benefits sanction.

Participants' accounts of their experiences were analysed using IPA and this process identified three superordinate themes: 1. Life Lived in Shades of Grey, 2. Good Citizen, Bad Citizen, and 3. Helping Hands. Key findings are now discussed with reference to the literature, and unique contributions of this research are highlighted. The methodological strengths and limitations of the research are then discussed, before the implications for future research.

5.2 Key Findings

This study has provided rich, deep insight into the process of living with complex mental health difficulties during a benefits sanction. The accounts present were generated from individuals with direct lived experience of this situation, and this research supports the view that providing context to individuals' experiences of distress, and emphasising the subjective and unique meanings of these experiences, can improve our understanding of this set of complex circumstances. While also acknowledging this complexity, important patterns found in the individuals' experiences emerged, which can now be discussed further.

5.2.1 Life Lived in Shades of Grey

Rather than expressing the need or want of an individual to have their lives and situation set out on black and white, the findings from the first superordinate theme highlight a range of feelings and motivations around having the nuances of their lives all but ignored by the DWP. One primary view was that societal views, and the DWP through welfare conditionality, were punishing them for life situations out with of their control. The individuals in this research described their difficulties in interacting and dealing with wider narratives and beliefs around benefit claimants and 'mental illness', and a system that forces compliment behaviour through penalising and harsh methods, which presented in various forms, including; arbitrary sanction decisions, negative DWP staff attitudes and wider societal views on those 'deserving' to be sanctioned, all of which bred feelings of worthlessness, loss of control, shame, and entrapment. This eagerness to breed compliancy and change claimants into 'model citizens' through benefit sanctions and subsequent employment, in regardless of personal circumstance, has a dearth of positive evidence behind it (Watts et al, 2014). Welfare conditionality in the face of dire personal and social issues in fact negatively impacts on chances of moving into work, and an increase in poor mental health (Patrick, 2014; 2017).

This finding is consistent with the previous literature, and in particular PAA's work around the harmful psychological impacts of austerity in the system (PAA, 2015; Shakespeare, 2017). The findings raised from the first superordinate theme also give empirical support to the evidence that welfare-to-work rhetoric forced on claimants, especially after a sanction, in fact undermines the development of a supportive and productive relationship between claimant and job centre that would actually result in a healthy individual in meaningful employment (Dwyer et al, 2016; Wright, 2016).

These findings may also be suggestive of the significant and pressing material and symbolic hardship a benefit sanction can cause, often creating more barriers for the individual becoming meaningfully well, physically, mentally, and socially in order to then choose beneficial, and importantly, wanted employment. This is evident from findings, and also supports previous findings by Batty and colleagues, who found the more pushed the individual is towards being forced to survive destitution brought on by welfare compliance tactics, such as a benefits sanction, the less time is spent on becoming mentally well, and as a result less time spent actively seeking meaningful employment and complying with DWP procedures (Fitzpatrick et al, 2016; Batty et al, 2016). Subsequently, the welfare conditionality regime pushed by the DWP, government, and in ways by wider society, has the perverse consequence of undermining mental, physical, and social wellness of individuals in need, further supporting findings by PAA in their recent paper on the impacts of austerity (PAA, 2015; McKee, 2017). The DWP's emphasis on conditionality and sanctions shown by this study's research findings are illogical considering the hetegenerous nature of the group, who are already busy with the work of managing sudden and increasing deprivation, worsening mental health, and fragmented social support, all brought on by the sanction itself, and wider welfare reforms (Halpern, 2014; Martin-Carrasco et al, 2016; Patrick, 2017).

Findings here have shown the rationale behind conditionality measures need to be reconsidered, and attention paid to just how much current welfare provision for those with mental health difficulties – disclosed or not – provided is fit for purpose (McKee, 2017; O'Hara, 2014; Loopstra et al, 2015).

5.2.2 Good Citizen, Bad Citizen

Participants described significant adversity in their early lives recently, with one dealing with it since childhood. It is possible that these experiences may have given rise to particular vulnerabilities and views regarding themselves, their situation, and their place in wider society (Briant et al, 2011; Geigar et al, 2017). T. H. Marshall's theory of citizenship frames these findings particularly well. He described social citizenship as the promise of equal status for all (Marshall, 1950). Social rights were considered the cornerstone of providing the required 'modicum of economic welfare and security' to those experiencing destitution and poverty (Dwyer, 2010). However, the numerous changes and ritualization have forced individuals to comply with state and societal-defined behaviours of conditionality, to show themselves to be 'deserving', worthy, healthy, and productive members of society, which the individuals taking part in this research continually found their poor mental health excluded them from (Leisering et al, 2013; Fraser, 2003; Thill, 2015). Findings found here also support previous research around welfare conditionality, that it is rarely welcomed, and often leads to feelings of lack of personal agency, control, and choice further hampered during the sanction period in particular (Slater, 2014; Marni et al, 2015). This research found this could lead to feelings of powerlessness, fear, and anger that only furthers feelings of insecurity in an already unstable and rapidly evolving situation, again, also found in the recent work carried out by Psychologists Against Austerity, and China Mills (PAA, 2015; Mills, 2017).

Participants' accounts also evidenced a narrowing of their personal perspectives around their situation, and also of treatment endured at the hands of the DWP and other organisations or wider society when their sanction period or mental health became particularly difficult, often together

(Barnes et al, 2016; Garthwaite, 2014). The nature of the participants' views of their 'citizenship status' and place in society increasingly became conditional on length and depth of interactions as a benefits claimant (Clarke et al, 2014); with thoughts and feelings around worthiness tied and contingent on successful completion of state-defined demands in order to be considered a 'good citizen' (Lister, 2011; Dwyer et al, 2014; Galston, 2005). The participants in this study also portrayed increasing acceptance of these societal expectations, increasingly interweaving them with their own internal views of their personal value, particularly around the idea of personal responsibility for the physical, mental, and social situation they find themselves in during their sanction period (Newman, 2011; Earle, 2017). In some ways, this seemed to lead to self-governing behaviours, engaging in activities that can be seen by wider society as them making an effort to turn from 'bad' to 'good' citizens, such as William's self-employment, Robert's detox and rehab, and Aaron's recovery (Dwyer et al, 2009; McKee, 2017; Patrick, 2017).

The idea that welfare conditionality is reliant on socially enforced stigma around claiming and being sanctioned as an actual tool of governance, supports the findings of this research (Tyler, 2014). Governance through stigma, either by oneself or by society, was evidenced throughout by the participants' thoughts, feelings, and action around getting mentally well and off benefits (Schram et al, 2008). Looking at findings from this research, coupled with previous findings from the literature, it can be seen that individuals faced with the double stigma surrounding benefit claims, sanctions, and poor mental health are becoming increasingly conditioned in the face of a dominant societal narrative concerned with their supposed irresponsible and reckless behaviour choices. As has been seen, as this conditioning continues throughout their interactions with the benefits system, their anger and self-blaming for a situation that is increasingly out of their control either turns inwards to chips away at their self-worth (Economou et al, 2013), further exacerbating their struggles with poor mental health, or turns outwards to be directed at the behaviours of other citizens seen as more deserving of a sanction, furthering exclusion and bolstering the work of stigmatisation as a form of welfare conditionality (Walker, 2014; PAA, 2015).

5.2.3 Helping Hands

Participants' accounts also shed light on the impact of benefit sanctions on their daily lives, and their mental health in particular, a heavy burden to carry when also living with fast-paced welfare changes and associated imposed hardship and insecurity. This burden has also been seen to undermine successful transitions from benefits to meaningful life goals, employment or not. Although for the participants here, employment was tied up in what they considered a personal meaningful and successful life goal. This fracturing of the system, with villainization of mental health difficulties in particular leading to a lack of empathy and support provided by the DWP and other services, has only served to make life harder for claimants who are often forced to survive and take care of themselves on their own, supporting previous findings by Fletcher and colleagues (2017), and others (Clement et al, 2015; Funk, 2016).

The burden of welfare reform and increased conditionality has had a knock-on effect on wider social security infrastructure in which individuals in the same situation as the participants would often turn to in times of physical, social and, most of all, mental health need. From social work offices, third sector food banks, and mental health crisis teams, the negative impact of an increase penalising system can be seen in the pressures the services face, with little help trickling down to those who need it (Lee et al, 2017; Dugan, 2014). This has led the participants in this particular research to reply on what society would judge to be negative and unhelping coping behaviours in the form their self-medicating choices took, furthering their isolation (Pickett et al, 2010; Cowley et al, 2016; PAA, 2015). The small costs judged to be saved by sanctioning these individuals is, on examination, far outstripped by subsequent costs on services through the horrendously negative impact it had on the participants' physical and mental health (Garthwaite, 2016), fulfilling a vicious cycle of service pressure, individuals at breaking point, and increasing benefit sanctions. As found through this research's findings, it may be that the only 'benefit' of an increasingly harsh welfare system and the use of benefit sanctions is that, in making the individuals so much harder, it forces a transition at some point, either to work, or out of the system, which in the eyes of the DWP is a success (Garrett, 2015). For the participants, being able to claw their way back from rock bottom, through self-care of any means (Cotti et al, 2015; Jackson et al, 2009), has enabled them to see a future beyond their experiences of the benefits system, a lucky occurrence that so many simply do not reach in a system that kills (Hasson-Ohayon et al, 2011; Mills, 2016).

5.3 Research Strengths and Limitations

These findings are based on a small sample of individuals who agreed to be interviewed. The study represents the experiences of this particular group who took part, and are therefore suggestive rather than conclusive with respect to their generalisability. The participants within this research were unique individuals in their personalities, backgrounds and experiences, as evidenced by the complex and nuanced nature of the data gathered. However, the relative homogeneity in the sample with respect to complex mental health difficulties and experience of a benefit sanction help to identify features that are specific to other individuals with these characteristics; but this requires further empirical examination in both similar and divergent samples.

The time and number of benefit sanctions varied within the sample from occurring more than a year ago, to still ongoing at time of interview, giving rise to the possibility that their accounts could be subject to retrospective biases, and that these recollections accommodated new experiences and insights not previously encountered, supporting Podskoff and Organ's (1986) suggestion that self-reported recall in different timespans can be subject to distortion and bias, and not easy to solve. However, Berney and colleagues (1997) argued that events recalled some time after the original time period can still remain useful, retain accuracy and benefit from personal reflection (Kendler et al, 2017; Patrick, 2017). Smith, Flowers, and Larkin (2009) recommend a homogenous sample, and as such it can be argued the differing recall periods between participants, even of a similar situation, could be too much of a difference. However, this slight violation of strict homogeneity allowed some interesting thoughts and views around the individual sense-making process of their unique situations, hopefully highlighting the importance of lived experience of dealing with complex mental health difficulties during a benefit sanction remains valid and important, regardless of how long ago that situation was experienced.

The interpretative facet of this research is viewed as a strength and important in relation to the original contribution of this study. The researcher actively participated in constructing the aims and research questions; design of the study; and interpretation of the data. In addition, the data itself is a product of the interaction between the researcher, who also has similar lived experience, and the participants, and as such, alternative interpretations of the findings are plausible.

Importantly, this study represents an exploration of the experiences dealing with complex mental health difficulties during a benefits sanction and survived. It is possible that there are important differences between individuals with a long history of complex mental health difficulties and experiences of suicidality during the sanction period, as was the case in the current study, and those who experienced the same situation, and have died by suicide (Mills, 2017).

5.4 Future Research

The discussion has highlighted important areas for future research. Further qualitative research in particular may be capable of shedding further light on; interactions, thoughts, and feelings with third party services aimed at improving mental health during a sanction period, contextualising and exploring the role of suicidal thoughts during the sanction period in particular, specifically in relation to financial, emotional, and life stressors, and exploring and contextualising the impact of 'criminal' and negative health behaviours as coping mechanisms for mental and life stressors during a benefits sanction. Of particular importance would be the targeted exploration of experiences of mental health and benefit claimant stigma perpetuated by the services themselves, and subsequent impact in clinically-engaged samples. Wider research of how broader practices by government agencies and political rhetoric affect the delivery and experience of wider social security for individuals with mental health difficulties is also a pressing future research concern, and should be explored.

5.5 Conclusions

This study explored how individuals with lived experience of complex mental health difficulties during a benefit sanction made sense of their experiences. Participants' accounts were dominated by experience of significant social adversity and psychological suffering, with feelings of isolation, marginalisation and internal and external stigma common.

Participants reflected on their often long-term and ongoing battles with poor mental health, and protracted relationship with the welfare system, providing rich, unique, and insightful accounts of their personal experiences. This highlights the inherent value of undertaking qualitative research with individuals with lived experience often denied a voice.

Given the unique, nuanced, individualized, and overall highly complex nature of their mental health difficulties and situations surrounding their sanction period, it is not possible to arrive at a definitive answer. However, important patterns in individuals' experiences were identified by the study in relation to 1. The overlooked nuances of everyday life by services, 2. Societal pressures in relation to internal and external stigma around benefit claimants, and 3. The situations leading up to, and usefulness of self-care, in relation to physical, social, and most importantly, mental health. Further empirical investigation of these themes and their components is indicated in order to directly inform future efforts.

6. Reflexivity

Within research utilizing the IPA framework, the result is a product of interaction between the researcher, the participants, and the data. In order for the meaning behind the participants sense-making to be unravelled, the researcher needs to be able to interpret and interact with subsequent generated data on a deep level. In turn, this interpretation is based on the researcher's own personal understanding, expectations, beliefs, and experiences of the situation being experienced by their participants. Therefore, personal reflexivity, and reflection throughout the research process is highly recommended in the IPA process (Smith et al, 2009). Reflecting on the ways in which personal values, experiences, and beliefs could have shaped the research is an important facet to understand subsequent data generation and theorisation (Willig, 2001). Furthermore, there is growing support within the wider social sciences for research to be inclusive and participatory to allow for a much more nuanced understanding of participants' sense-making of lived experiences within the context of a changing social, economic, and political climate (Williams et al, 2013). As such, the researcher having lived experience of the exact situation in which the participants also found themselves in could only improve the quality of analysis, research impact, and credibility of findings (Mjøsund et al, 2016).

I do believe my own experiences as a benefit claimant who was also sanctioned at a time in my life in which I was also struggling with severe and complex mental health difficulties did shape this research. My own experiences of stigma and support during this time have also been less than pleasant, which is why I am so passionate about bringing about change. I believe these personal feelings influenced by own sense-making of the participants' sense- making of their own experiences, resulting in the super- and subordinate themes subsequently found. This research was also influenced by a profoundly negative experience with a participant who was subsequently removed after police involvement for sexual assault. This had an understandable negative impact on me, which I strove to keep from affecting the research. I continued on to a second interview that day, and I am aware this experience affected all subsequent interviews, although, I am glad to say, not too much. After time to recover, I found coming back to the research took longer than usual to immerse myself in the data again, obviously a key step in the IPA process. It led me to consider researcher safety and the space often given over to the very real harms we, as researchers, can have on our participants, and in comparison, the very little space given over to the harms our participants can do to us in turn. All of this will be kept in mind and carried forward into any future research.

Bibliography

Abdullah, T. and Brown, T.L., 2011. Mental illness stigma and ethnocultural beliefs, values, and norms: An integrative review. *Clinical psychology review*, 31(6), pp.934-948.

Alonso J, Angermeyer MC, Bernert S, Bruffaerts R, Brugha T, Bryson H, Girolamo G, Graaf R, Demyttenaere K, Gasquet I: Use of mental health services in Europe: results from the European Study of the Epidemiology of Mental Disorders (ESEMeD) project. *Acta Psychiatr Scand. 2004*, 109 (s420): 47-54.

Andrews G, Sanderson K, Slade T, Issakidis C: Why does the burden of disease persist? Relating the burden of anxiety and depression to effectiveness of treatment. *Bull World Health Organ*. 2000, 78 (4): 446-454.

Arni, P., Lalive, R. and Van Ours, J.C., 2013. How effective are unemployment benefit sanctions? Looking beyond unemployment exit. *Journal of applied econometrics*, 28(7), pp.1153-1178.

Authority, U.S., 2015. Benefit Sanction Statistics. *Response to FOI request, made by Chair of the UK Statistics Authority, Sir Andrew Dilnot CBE)*, 5(8), p.15.

Bambra, C., & Garthwaite, K. (2015). Austerity, welfare reform and the English health divide. *Area, 47*(3), 341-343.

Branas, C. C., Kastanaki, A. E., Michalodimitrakis, M., Tzougas, J., Kranioti, E. F., Theodorakis, P. N., ... & Wiebe, D. J. (2015). The impact of economic austerity and prosperity events on suicide in Greece: a 30-year interrupted time-series analysis. *BMJ open, 5*(1), e005619.

Barnes, M.C., Gunnell, D., Davies, R., Hawton, K., Kapur, N., Potokar, J. and Donovan, J.L., 2016. Understanding vulnerability to self-harm in times of economic hardship and austerity: a qualitative study. *BMJ open, 6*(2), p. e010131.

Berney, L.R. and Blane, D.B., 1997. Collecting retrospective data: accuracy of recall after 50 years judged against historical records. *Social science & medicine, 45*(10), pp.1519-1525.

Brown, J.S., Evans-Lacko, S., Aschan, L., Henderson, M.J., Hatch, S.L. and Hotopf, M., 2014. Seeking informal and formal help for mental health problems in the community: a secondary analysis from a psychiatric morbidity survey in South London. *BMC psychiatry, 14*(1), p.275.

Clement, S., Schauman, O., Graham, T., Maggioni, F., Evans-Lacko, S., Bezborodovs, N., Morgan, C., Rüsch, N., Brown, J.S.L. and Thornicroft, G., 2015. What is the impact of mental health-related stigma on help-seeking? A systematic review of quantitative and qualitative studies. *Psychological medicine, 45*(1), pp.11-27.

Conrad, P., 2010. *Deviance and medicalization: From badness to sickness*. Temple University Press.

Corbin, J. and Morse, J.M., 2003. The unstructured interactive interview: Issues of reciprocity and risks when dealing with sensitive topics. *Qualitative inquiry, 9*(3), pp.335- 354.

Corcoran, P., Griffin, E., Arensman, E., Fitzgerald, A. P., & Perry, I. J. (2015). Impact of the economic recession and subsequent austerity on suicide and self-harm in Ireland: An interrupted time series analysis. *International journal of epidemiology, 44*(3), 969-977.

Cotti, C., Dunn, R.A. and Tefft, N., 2015. The Dow is killing me: risky health behaviors and the stock market. *Health economics, 24*(7), pp.803-821.

Cowley, J., Kiely, J. and Collins, D., 2016. Unravelling the Glasgow effect: The relationship between accumulative bio-psychosocial stress, stress reactivity and Scotland's health problems. *Preventive medicine reports*, 4, pp.370-375.

Creswell, J.W. and Poth, C.N., 2017. *Qualitative inquiry and research design: Choosing among five approaches*. Sage publications.

Cross, M., 2013. Demonised, impoverished and now forced into isolation: the fate of disabled people under austerity. *Disability & Society, 28*(5), pp.719-723.

De Choudhury, M., Gamon, M., Counts, S. and Horvitz, E., 2013. Predicting Depression via Social Media. *ICWSM, 13*, pp.1-10.

Dwyer, P. and Bright, J., 2016. Welfare Conditionality: Sanctions, support and behavioral change. *University of Glasgow*.

Dwyer, P. and Wright, S., 2014. Universal credit, ubiquitous conditionality and its implications for social citizenship. *Journal of Poverty and Social Justice, 22*(1), pp.27-35.

Dwyer, P., 2010. *Understanding social citizenship: Themes and perspectives for policy and practice*. Policy press.

Dwyer, P.J. and Ellison, N., 2009. *Work and welfare: the rights and responsibilities of unemployment in the UK*.

Earle, L., 2017. Housing, Citizenship and the Right to the City. In *Transgressive Citizenship and the Struggle for Social Justice* (pp. 27-64). Springer International Publishing.

Economou, M., Madianos, M., Peppou, L.E., Patelakis, A. and Stefanis, C.N., 2013. Major depression in the era of economic crisis: a replication of a cross-sectional study across Greece. *Journal of Affective Disorders, 145*(3), pp.308-314.

Erikson, K.T., 2003. On the sociology of deviance. *Constructions of deviance: Social power, context, and interaction*, pp.11-18.

Fisher, E.B., Fitzgibbon, M.L., Glasgow, R.E., Haire-Joshu, D., Hayman, L.L., Kaplan, R.M., Nanney, M.S. and Ockene, J.K., 2011. Behavior matters. *American journal of preventive medicine, 40*(5), pp. e15-e30.

Fitzpatrick, T., 2004. Time, social justice and UK welfare reform. *Economy and society, 33*(3), pp.335-358.

Fletcher, D.R., 2011. Welfare reform, Jobcentre Plus and the street-level bureaucracy: towards inconsistent and discriminatory welfare for severely disadvantaged groups? *Social policy and Society, 10*(4), pp.445-458.

Franklin K (2013) *Investigating the real reason for the misery of 'fit for work' assessment.* Retrieved June 2017: http://www.centreforwelfarereform.org/uploads/attachment/400/how- norms- become-targets.pdf.

Freeman, L., 2008. Recognition reconsidered: Leaping ahead toward a Heideggerian approach. In *Proceedings of the 42nd annual North American Heidegger conference.*

Funk, M., 2016. *Global burden of mental disorders and the need for a comprehensive, coordinated response from health and social sectors at the country level.*

Gallie, D., Felstead, A., Green, F. and Inanc, H., 2017. The hidden face of job insecurity. *Work, employment and society, 31*(1), pp.36-53.

Galston, W., 2005. Conditional citizenship. *Welfare reform and political theory*, pp.110-26.

Garrett, P.M., 2015. Words matter: deconstructing 'welfare dependency 'in the UK. *Critical and Radical Social Work, 3*(3), pp.389-406.

Garthwaite, K., 2014. Fear of the Brown Envelope: Exploring Welfare Reform with Long Term Sickness Benefits Recipients. *Social Policy & Administration, 48*(7), pp.782-798.

Garthwaite, K., 2016. *Hunger pains: Life inside foodbank Britain.* Policy Press.

Gaventa, J., 2016. *Can Participation 'fix 'Inequality? Unpacking the Relationship Between the Economic and Political Citizenship.*

Halpern, D., 2014. *Mental health and the built environment: more than bricks and mortar?* Routledge.

Harrison, J., 2014. Two-Way Street: The Textures of Living in Merleau-Ponty. *Self & Society, 41*(3), pp.28-32.

Hasson-Ohayon, I., Levy, I., Kravetz, S., Vollanski-Narkis, A. and Roe, D., 2011. Insight into mental illness, self-stigma, and the family burden of parents of persons with a severe mental illness. *Comprehensive Psychiatry, 52*(1), pp.75-80.

Haw, C., Hawton, K., Gunnell, D., & Platt, S. (2015). Economic recession and suicidal behaviour: Possible mechanisms and ameliorating factors. *International Journal of Social Psychiatry, 61*(1), 73-81.

Hayim, G., 2017. *Existentialism and Sociology: Contribution of Jean-Paul Sartre*. Routledge.

Husserl, E., 2012. Ideas: *General introduction to pure phenomenology*. Routledge.

Heidegger, M., 1988. *The basic problems of phenomenology* (Vol. 478). Indiana University Press.

Jackson, J.S., Knight, K.M. and Rafferty, J.A., 2010. Race and unhealthy behaviors: chronic stress, the HPA axis, and physical and mental health disparities over the life course. *American journal of public health, 100*(5), pp.933-939.

Jacob, S.A. and Furgerson, S.P., 2012. Writing interview protocols and conducting interviews: Tips for students new to the field of qualitative research. *The Qualitative Report, 17*(42), pp.1-10.

Karanikolos, M., Heino, P., McKee, M., Stuckler, D., & Legido-Quigley, H. (2016). Effects of the global financial crisis on health in high-income Oecd countries: a narrative review. *International journal of health services, 46*(2), 208-240.

Karanikolos, M., Mladovsky, P., Cylus, J., Thomson, S., Basu, S., Stuckler, D., Mackenbach, J.P. and McKee, M., 2013. Financial crisis, austerity, and health in Europe. *The Lancet, 381*(9874), pp.1323-1313

Karp, J.F., Kleinman, A., Reynolds III, C.F., Weiner, D.K. and Cleary, P.D., 2013. Older People's Experiences of Patient-Centered Treatment for Chronic Pain: A Qualitative Study. *Pain medicine, 10*(3), pp.521-530.

Kendler, K.S. and Gardner, C.O., 2017. Genetic and environmental influences on last-year major depression in adulthood: a highly heritable stable liability but strong environmental effects on 1-year prevalence. *Psychological Medicine*, pp.1-9.

Lee, C., Hartley, C. and Sharland, E., 2017. Risk thinking and the priorities of mental health social work organizations. *Beyond the Risk Paradigm in Mental Health Policy and Practice*, p.30.

Leisering, L. and Barrientos, A., 2013. Social citizenship for the global poor? The worldwide spread of social assistance. *International Journal of Social Welfare, 22*(S1).

Lister, S., Reynolds, L. and Webb, K., 2011. *Research report the impact of welfare reform bill measures on affordability for low income private renting families*.

Marmot, M. and Bell, R., 2012. Fair society, healthy lives. *Public health, 126*, pp. S4-S10.

Marshall, T.H., 1950. *Citizenship and social class* (Vol. 11, pp. 28-29). Cambridge.

Martin-Carrasco, M., Evans-Lacko, S., Dom, G., Christodoulou, N. G., Samochowiec, J., Gonzalez-Fraile, E., ... & Wasserman, D. (2016). EPA guidance on mental health and economic crises in Europe. *European archives of psychiatry and clinical neuroscience, 266*(2), 89-124.

Mattheys, K., Bambra, C., Warren, J., Kasim, A., & Akhter, N. (2016). Inequalities in mental health and well-being in a time of austerity: Baseline findings from the Stockton-On-Tees cohort study. *SSM-Population Health, 2*, 350-359.

McCarthy, L., Batty, E., Beatty, C., Casey, R., Foden, M. and Reeve, K.,

2015. *Homeless people's experiences of welfare conditionality and benefit sanctions*.

McCartney, G., Russ, T.C., Walsh, D., Lewsey, J., Smith, M., Smith, G.D., Stamatakis, E. and Batty, G.D., 2014. Explaining the excess mortality in Scotland compared with England: pooling of 18 cohort studies. *J Epidemiol Community Health*, pp. jech-2014.

McGarth, L., Griffin, V., & Mundy, E. (2015). *The Psychological Impact of Austerity: A briefing paper*. United Kingdom: Psychologists Against Austerity. Available at http://www.psychchange.org/uploads/9/7/9/7/97971280/paa-briefing-paper.pdf [Accessed: 19/09/2017].

McKee, M., 2017. *Grenfell Tower fire: why we cannot ignore the political determinants of health*.

McKee, M., Karanikolos, M., Belcher, P. and Stuckler, D., 2012. Austerity: a failed experiment on the people of Europe. *Clinical medicine, 12*(4), pp.346-350.

McNeill, J.M., Jones, K., Scullion, L. and Stewart, A., 2017. Welfare conditionality and disabled people in the UK: claimants' perspectives. *The Journal of Poverty and Social Justice*, pp.177-180.

Merleau-Ponty, M., 2017. Phenomenology and Its Shadow: Visuality in the Late Work of Merleau-Ponty. *The Handbook of Visual Culture*, p.115.

Mjøsund, N.H., Eriksson, M., Haaland-Øverby, M., Jensen Liang, S., Norheim, I., Espnes, G.A. and Forbech Vinje, H., 2016. Salutogenic Service User Involvement: Experiences from Collaboration between an Advisory Team and Researchers in a Mental Health Research Project. *International Journal of Consumer Studies*.

Newman, I., 2011. Work as a route out of poverty: a critical evaluation of the UK welfare to work policy. *Policy Studies, 32*(2), pp.91-108.

Novoa, A.M., Ward, J., Malmusi, D., Díaz, F., Darnell, M., Trilla, C., Bosch, J. and Borrell, C., 2015. How substandard dwellings and housing affordability problems are associated with poor health in a vulnerable population during the economic recession of the late 2000s. *International journal for equity in health, 14*(1), p.120.

O'Hara M., 2014. *Austerity Bites: a journey to the sharp end of cuts in the UK*. Bristol, Policy Press.

ONS., 2015. *Suicides in the United Kingdom, 2013 registrations*. London: Office for National Statistics.

Osborn, M. and Smith, J.A., 2008. The fearfulness of chronic pain and the centrality of the therapeutic relationship in containing it: an interpretative phenomenological analysis. *Qualitative Research in Psychology, 5*(4), pp.276-288.

Patrick, R. (2016). Living with and responding to the 'scrounger' narrative in the UK: exploring everyday strategies of acceptance, resistance and deflection. *Journal of Poverty and Social Justice, 24*(3), 245-259.

Patrick, R., 2017. *For whose benefit? The everyday realities of welfare reform*. Policy Press.

Pernice-Duca, F., 2010. Family network support and mental health recovery. *Journal of Marital and Family Therapy, 36*(1), pp.13-27.

Piccoli, B. and De Witte, H., 2015. Job insecurity and emotional exhaustion: Testing psychological contract breach versus distributive injustice as indicators of lack of reciprocity. *Work & Stress, 29*(3), pp.246-263.

Pickett, K.E. and Wilkinson, R.G., 2010. *Inequality: an underacknowledged source of mental illness and distress*.

Pietkiewicz, I. and Smith, J.A., 2014. A practical guide to using interpretative phenomenological analysis in qualitative research psychology. *Psychological Journal, 20*(1), pp.7-14.

Pitschel-Walz, G., Leucht, S., Bäuml, J., Kissling, W. and Engel, R.R., 2015. The effect of family interventions on relapse and rehospitalization in schizophrenia: a meta-analysis. *Focus*.

Podsakoff, P.M. and Organ, D.W., 1986. Self-reports in organizational research: Problems and prospects. *Journal of management, 12*(4), pp.531-544.

Psychologists, A. A, 2015. *The psychological impact of austerity: A briefing paper. Retrieved November, 2016.* United Kingdom: Psychologists for Social Change. Available at http://www.psychchange.org/uploads/9/7/9/7/97971280/paa-briefing-paper.pdf. [Accessed 19/09/2017].

Rambotti, S., 2015. Recalibrating the spirit level: An analysis of the interaction of income inequality and poverty and its effect on health. *Social Science & Medicine, 139*, pp.123-131.

Repper, J. and Carter, T., 2011. A review of the literature on peer support in mental health services. *Journal of Mental Health, 20*(4), pp.392-411.

Richardson, T., Elliott, P. and Roberts, R., 2013. The relationship between personal unsecured debt and mental and physical health: a systematic review and meta-analysis. *Clinical psychology review, 33*(8), pp.1148-1162.

Sartre, J.P., 2012. *Being and nothingness*. Open Road Media.

Schram, S.F., Fording, R.C. and Soss, J., 2008. Neo-liberal poverty governance: Race, place and the punitive turn in US welfare policy. *Cambridge journal of regions, economy and society, 1*(1), pp.17-36.

Shakespeare, T., Watson, N. and Alghaib, O.A., 2017. Blaming the victim, all over again: Waddell and Aylward's biopsychosocial (BPS) model of disability. *Critical Social Policy, 37*(1), pp.22-41.

Slater, T., 2014. The myth of "Broken Britain": welfare reform and the production of ignorance. *Antipode, 46*(4), pp.948-969.

Sloan, C., Gough, B. and Conner, M., 2010. Healthy masculinities? How ostensibly healthy men talk about lifestyle, health and gender. *Psychology and Health, 25*(7), pp.783-803.

Smith, J., Flowers, P. and Larkin, M., 2009. *Interpretative Phoneomological*

Analysis: theory, method and research. Sage.

Smith, J.A., Harré, R. and Van Langenhove, L. eds., 1995. *Rethinking methods in psychology*. Sage.

Social Research Association, 2006. A code of practice for the safety of social researchers. *Retrieved October, 9*, p.2007.

Stanford Encyclopaedia of Philosophy, 2017. *Hermeneutics*. [Online]. Available at: https://plato.stanford.edu/entries/hermeneutics. [Accessed 23 September 2017].

Taylor, C., 1985. *Human agency and language*. London.

Thill, C., 2015. Listening for policy change: how the voices of disabled people shaped Australia's National Disability Insurance Scheme. *Disability & Society, 30*(1), pp.15-28.

Tyler, I., 2014. *From 'The Shock Doctrine' to 'The Stigma Doctrine'*.

Walker, R. and Bantebya-Kyomuhendo, G., 2014. *The shame of poverty*. Oxford University Press, USA.

Walsh, D., Bendel, N., Jones, R. and Hanlon, P., 2010. *Investigating a 'Glasgow Effect': why do equally deprived UK cities experience different health outcomes?*

Walsh, D., McCartney, G., Collins, C., Taulbut, M. and Batty, G.D., 2017. History, politics and vulnerability: explaining excess mortality in Scotland and Glasgow. *Public Health, 151*, pp.1-12.

Watts, B., Fitzpatrick, S., Bramley, G. and Watkins, D., 2014. *Welfare Sanctions and Conditionality in the UK*. Joseph Rowntree Foundation.

Whyte, B. and Ajetunmobi, T., 2012. *Still" the Sick Man of Europe"? Scottish Mortality in a European Context, 1950-2010: An Analysis of Comparative Mortality Trends*. Glasgow Centre for Population Health.

Williams, G.A. and Zlotowitz, S., 2013. Using a community psychology approach in your research. *PsyPAG Quarterly*, (86), pp.21-25.

Willig, C., 2001. *Qualitative research in psychology: A practical guide to theory and method*. Buckingham: OUP.

Wright, S., 2016. Conceptualising the active welfare subject: welfare reform in discourse, policy and lived experience. *Policy & Politics, 44*(2), pp.235-252.

Appendix A: Dissertation Interview Schedule Themes

Demographics

1. Age, gender, mental health condition (?), type of benefit they are on, how long been on it, number of times sanctioned

Being on benefits

1. Potted history
2. Particularly challenging moments, experience of job centers
- PROMPT: originally signing on, proving status, PIP, sanctions

Experiences of sanctions

1. How many times been sanctioned?
2. Focus on last experience: events leading up to it, how long, how did it affect you?
- PROMPT: debt, physical health, mental health

Mental health

1. I'd like to explore in a bit more detail the impact of benefit sanctions on your MH.
- PROMPT: management, daily living, interactions with professionals

Support & self-care

1. What did you do to get by during your sanction period?
2. What does self-care mean to you?
3. How did you make yourself feel better during this time?
- PROMPT: food bank, loans, friends + family, effects of self-care on MH

Closing question

1. Based on your experience, what is the most important thing that mental health professionals, or anyone, should know in order to be helpful to people with poor mental health in the benefits system?

Appendix B: Sample Transcripts

WILLIAM: Always like, 'arseholes!' [*laughs*]. That sort of stuff. Can't say that sort of thing anymore.	*Society constantly reinforces SES position, EG. Poor people can only afford to eat crap, and looked down upon for it?*
INTERVIEWER: Eh, yeah so, I wanted to ask... like we were touching on earlier- the whole recovery- the idea that you can recover fully-	
W.: Well, I think they sell you that idea and say, *"Take these pills, and you'll be back to normal"*. Yeah, yeah, I don't believe in that. I don't believe in that, doesn't work. It doesn't work, but in their defence, they've- maybe it's better for some people who've got mental health issues that are quite prone to violence or- well destructive. Or would kill themselves, then yeah... they should- prescriptions and pills and medication should balance out what's good for the person, what's good for society. It never does, it's always what's good for society. Keep people medicated, keep them down. So, you can be shown to be 'good'. So, when you come off your medication, or have a bad time, you're somehow 'bad'.	*Recovery just another way to try and make you a good citizen?* *Drs give you pills to make you 'normal' in societies eyes.* *For some people this is how they cope?* *Never good for individual person, always in interest of wider society.*
I.: That feeds into-	
W.: Benefit scrounger thingy. Yeah, urgh,and I hate that term! I hate that term!	*On benefits, DWP and have been sanctioned, considered bad, and scrounger?*

I.: That's what-	
W.: I'm quite sure there are some people who do. But... all these people have tarred everyone on benefits with the same brush. I was seeing on Facebook about a girl who was in a top floor flat and she couldn't walk, had issues. And they wouldn't give her a ground floor flat! Did you not see it? Fucking awful!	*DWP/society tar everyone with same brush who are on benefits* *No compassion* *No understanding*

www.ingramcontent.com/pod-product-compliance
Lightning Source LLC
Chambersburg PA
CBHW071120030426
42336CB00013BA/2155